Red-Letter Language

BY
HOWARD WIGHT, CLU, ChFC

Wight Financial Concepts Corporation
1330 Jones Street, Suite 404
San Francisco, CA 94109
800-486-SELL

Dedication

To my children, David and Jennifer, whom I love very much, and who have paid a very high price for whatever success I may have achieved. And to Ben Feldman, who helped me believe in myself.

Acknowledgment

In addition to all the people whose ideas have formed the basis of this book, I would like to thank Debra Ackerman for her hard work, patience, and persistence.

Fourth edition.

Library of Congress Catalog Card Number: 93-93966
ISBN 0-9633506-2-5

TABLE OF CONTENTS

Introduction

The purpose of this book is to help you say the right things to the right people at the right time.

A picture can be worth a thousand words. Some words can be worth a thousand pictures. A few words, an idea, a concept, a new approach, a different perspective, can change a lifetime. This book is a potpourri of power phrases, capsule comments, and key concepts which I have collected over the years. Thanks to Ben Feldman and to the many others whose words are recorded here.

Power phrases are basically verbal 2 x 4's which have logical and emotional impact. They get your attention. Ideas open doors and minds and relationships. Open more doors, minds, and relationships, and you will close more sales.

The key to making more sales is to make more calls to more people who have more money. The ideas contained in this book will give you the ammunition you need to call, see, and sell more people. Adopt these ideas. Adapt them to your own personality. Then act on them.

Repetition, reinforcement, and reminders are the keys to learning, expertise, and mastery. There is a certain amount of repetition in order to demonstrate how some phrases can be used in different situations.

Carry this book with you in your pocket or your car. Review it frequently. Mark it up. Make notes. Change the wording, so that you feel comfortable using it. Good luck and good selling.

Howard Wight, CLU, ChFC
January 2002

Overview

THE CLOSING ATTITUDE

❏ This person is in a financial mess. Right now, I am the only person in the world who can help him. I can make a difference.

❏ I am doing far more for him, his family, and his business, than he is doing for me.

❏ Life insurance works. There is no substitute for it . . . not stocks, not bonds, not mutual funds, not real estate, not limited partnerships.

❏ There is no cost for having life insurance . . . only a cost for not having it.

❏ The premium is not the problem. The premium is the solution to the problem. The premium is always peanuts compared to the problem.

❑ Every problem is an opportunity.

❑ If this person cares, I will persist. Life is too short to work with people who don't care.

❑ I will assume consent. Until he stops me, I will go forward with the sale. I will ask him to buy. I will ask him for the check.

ASSUMING CONSENT

The most important concept to understand in order to generate bigger sales is that of assuming consent. Assume that you have a green light to proceed through the selling process without ever having the client say "yes" to each specific step along the way. You merely move from one step to the next. Your ability to do this should be facilitated by knowing that what you are doing is right for your client. There should be absolutely no reason why he would not want to do business with you.

In the preliminary meeting, you should just start asking the client questions rather than asking for his permission to do so. When you have pinpointed the problems, you can then say, "Why don't I put some ideas together so that you can take a look." Then set a time for your presentation appointment.

When you have shown him his options, you should assume that he wants to take action. The next logical step is to set a time for the medical examination. The next step is for him to okay the applications. Now all we need is a check. Would you rather pay annually or monthly?

❑ Success is about making a difference. You make a difference. People dream dreams. You help convert their dreams to reality. You help keep their dreams alive. Without enough life insurance, their dreams will die when they do.

❑ Focus on WII-FM (What's In It For Me) from the prospect's perspective. Make him aware of the cost of action and the greater cost of inaction. The premium is not the problem. The premium is the solution to the problem.

❑ Are you asking enough of the right people to buy enough?

❑ Rich people have more money than poor people.

❑ LESS = More. Combine Logic, Emotion, Simplification, and Sincerity.

❏ People want holes . . . not drills. They want to know what time it is . . . not how to build a clock.

❏ If they don't buy the concept . . . the details are irrelevant.

❏ Joint work is a fast track to success.

❏ Where is it written that you have to be perfect in order to help people?

❏ Pinpoint the problems. Then put price tags on the problems.

❏ People will tell you what you need to know about them once they know that you care about them.

Getting the
Appointment

Correction

❑ Good morning, Mr. Prospect. This is John Agent, with ABC Associates. Recently, I had an opportunity to work with your friend, Bob Referror, who suggested that we should meet. (Leave this out if you don't have a referral.)

I've had an opportunity (my associates and I have had an opportunity) to work with some of the most successful people here in the Bay Area. I would like to show you the type of work that I do and show you some of the ideas that other successful people (business owners) like yourself have found profitable.

When can you fit me into your schedule (for 20 minutes)?

❏ I'M NOT INTERESTED.

❏ Why is that?

❏ WHAT IS THIS ABOUT?

❏ We're involved in:
  ❏ Wealth creation planning
  ❏ Wealth conservation planning
  ❏ Business continuation planning
  ❏ Selective compensation planning
  It will take about twenty minutes to give you an overview. When can you fit me into your schedule?

❏ I DO MY OWN PLANNING.

❏ Are you your own doctor and attorney also? No one has covered all the bases. Missing just one base could cost you or your family millions of dollars. Wouldn't it make sense to get a second opinion? A second opinion almost always makes good sense, wouldn't you agree?

❏ I'VE BEEN THROUGH ALL THIS. I JUST REVIEWED EVERYTHING WITH MY ATTORNEY, MY AC-COUNTANT, MY STOCKBROKER, AND MY INSURANCE AGENT. I'M ALL SET.

❏ Let me suggest this to you. Most people today, if they were going to undergo major surgery, and they had time, would want to get a second opinion. A second opinion almost always makes good sense, wouldn't you agree? (Pause, but don't await a response because a second opinion does make good sense.) When can you fit me into your schedule for twenty minutes?

13

❏ I'M JUST TOO BUSY.

❏ Most successful people are so busy being successful that they don't have time to keep on top of all the changes in the tax law and in the financial marketplace.

To the extent they have done planning, they have typically done it on a piece-meal basis, getting different advice from different advisors at different times.

When was the last time you sat down with all of your advisors at one time? Why?

Most people have never had such a meeting or if they have, it was to discuss a specific issue or concern.

❑ I'M STILL JUST NOT INTERESTED.

❑ At the end of twenty minutes, if you feel I've wasted your time, I'll write my personal check for $100 to your favorite charity. Isn't that fair? (Pause, but don't await a response, because it is fair.) When can you fit me into your schedule?

❑ I APPRECIATE YOUR PERSIS-TENCE . . . BUT I'M STILL NOT INTERESTED.

❑ Circumstances change. Would you have any objection to my keeping in touch from time to time? If I may ask, what is your date of birth? I use that to trigger my follow-up calls. That way, we can save you some money.

❏ IF THIS IS ABOUT INSURANCE, I'M NOT INTERESTED.

❏ We're involved in overall insurance and financial planning, so of course, insurance is part of what we do . . . but it's just one part. You can benefit from my services even if you never buy one penny of life insurance. When can you fit me into your schedule?

❏ CAN YOU SEND ME SOMETHING IN THE MAIL WHICH EXPLAINS WHAT YOU DO?

❏ It would take a book to explain what takes me twenty minutes to explain using a diagram in person. When can you fit me into your schedule?

❏ WHAT DO YOU DO?

❏ I'm in the insurance and financial planning business. I specialize in working with successful people on both a personal and business basis. I help them coordinate their estate planning, their business continuation planning, and their selective compensation planning. When can you fit me into your schedule?

❏ I specialize in personal and business estate planning.

❏ I specialize in multigenerational family business planning.

❏ I help people become millionaires.

❏ I specialize in designing selective compensation plans for key executives.

17

❑ I specialize in coordinating life insurance with your overall financial planning.

❑ I help people save money and taxes.

❑ I help people create and conserve wealth.

❑ I help people buy life insurance.

❑ I help people make smart decisions regarding their money. Money is important to most people. Tell me, what's important about money to you?

❑ Most people are playing the game of life without a game plan. I help them develop a game plan . . . an overall Master Action Plan . . . a MAP to get them where they want to go.

MR. PROSPECT –

❑ Would you be interested in a plan which could:

   ❑ Reduce your current taxes

   ❑ Increase your income

   ❑ Give a substantial gift to charity in your name

   ❑ Leave more to your children

❑ Would you be open to reviewing your insurance (and investment) program (planning) with me? (This works, but you have to be willing to accept a lot of No's.)

GETTING PAST THE ASSISTANT

❑ The assistant is the power behind the throne. Be polite. You're trying to help

her boss. You are not the enemy.
Answer her questions. Don't be evasive.

❑ If you have a referral, getting through
to the boss should be no problem. You
might also drop the names of clients
who have given you permission to
do so.

❑ If the assistant becomes an obstacle,
try calling when she is not there, either
early in the morning or late in the
afternoon.

❑ WHAT IS THIS ABOUT?

❑ I help my clients make smart decisions
regarding their money (investments
and insurance). I specialize in designing business succession plans and
selective compensation plans for key
employees.

Facts, Feelings, and Questions

GENERAL APPROACH TALK

Mr. Prospect, insurance and financial planning boils down to four basic areas:
- ❏ Wealth creation
- ❏ Wealth conservation (estate planning)
- ❏ Business continuation planning
- ❏ Selective compensation planning

The problem most people have is that the planning they have done has generally been done in a piecemeal manner. They are getting different advice from different people, at different times. This inevitably results in hundreds of thousands of dollars, if not millions, going down the drain unnecessarily.

The best way I know for both of us to determine whether or not you can benefit from my services is for me to ask you some questions. (Move into the fact and feeling finding.)

ESTATE PLANNING APPROACH

Mr. Prospect, your estate is the tangible representation of your lifetime. Without proper prior planning, the IRS estate tax collector will ultimately take about 50% of everything you have spent a lifetime building. That just doesn't seem fair, does it?

❑ Could you write a check today for 50% of everything you own without it hurting just a little bit? If you can't write that check, how will your children be able to write it?

❑ What have you done to reduce the impact of estate taxes on your family and business?

❑ As a business person, if you knew that your family faced an inevitable expense which could be reduced by 80% or more, wouldn't you be interested in exploring that avenue?

❑ What have you done in terms of making gifts to your children or to your favorite charity in order to reduce the impact of estate taxes?

❑ Why don't I put together some ideas for you? All I need is some basic information. (Now move into fact and feeling finding.)

WHY DON'T WE TAKE A MINUTE
AND LET ME TELL YOU WHAT I DO,
HOW I DO IT, AND HOW I AM PAID.

❏ What I do is to coordinate your
personal and business insurance and
financial planning . . . getting into such
areas as:

    ❏ Wealth creation planning
    ❏ Wealth conservation planning
    ❏ Business continuation planning
    ❏ Selective compensation planning

❏ How do I do it? By asking questions
much as a doctor does when he is
getting your medical history. I will ask
you some questions so that we can
mutually determine whether or not you
can benefit from my services. Does
that approach make sense to you?

❏ How am I paid? I'm paid two ways. First, if there is a need for insurance or investments to accomplish your goals, I will recommend them. I am paid a commission on those. I would expect you to place the business through me. Is that fair?

Secondly, if you are pleased with the work that I have done, I would expect you to refer me to other successful, responsible people like yourself. Agreed?

❏ Do you have any questions or are there any special areas of interest that you would like to discuss?

❏ Tell me about yourself. How did you get where you are today?

❑ I'm not here to sell you anything today. All I would like to do is to ask you a few questions to see if you might have a need in the future for my services and products. Does that make sense?

❑ In terms of planning for your financial future, which area do you feel requires the most attention? Retirement planning? Estate planning? Business continuation planning? Selective compensation planning? Charitable giving? Education funding? Disability planning? Family income planning? Or is there any other area that you feel requires attention?

❑ May I show you an idea?

❏ May I show you an idea which many other successful business owners (individuals, executives, etc.) have found extremely useful in their overall planning?

❏ May I show you an idea which other successful people are using to save millions of dollars (in taxes)?

❏ If I can show you an idea that makes sense to you, will you do business with me?

❏ Would you have any objection to discussing your life insurance program with me?

❏ I can't create the need for life insurance. You either have a need based on your goals for your family, or you don't. Why don't I just ask you a few questions? (Assume consent and start asking.)

❏ How much are your tomorrows worth?

FINANCIAL FOCUS

❏ What are your plans regarding retirement? What are you doing to accomplish your plans?

❏ What types of investments do you favor? Why?

❏ What are your investment results over the past five years? Are you pleased?

❏ Would you be pleased with the same results over the next five years? What would you do differently?

❏ How much time do you spend selecting and managing your investments? How much is your time worth?

❏ What would happen to you and your family if your income were to stop today?

❑ What have you done to enable your family to have an adequate income in the event of your death?

❑ What role does life insurance play in your financial plans, both personally and in your business?

❑ To what extent are your spouse and children involved in your financial decision making?

❑ What advisors do you use and to what extent?

❑ What are your plans for your business at your retirement or death or disability?

❑ What steps have you taken to accomplish your plans for your business?

- ❏ To what extent are your children involved in your business?

- ❏ Who will ultimately run your business? What are you doing to retain and reward them?

- ❏ What are you doing in terms of selective compensation plans for yourself and your key people?

- ❏ What impact would your loss or the loss of key people have on your business (sales, profits, lines of credit)?

- ❏ How do you feel about your children receiving a large inheritance? Why?

- ❏ What is the potential estate tax impact and what have you done about it?

❑ To what extent have you made gifts to your children or considered doing so?

❑ What are your thoughts regarding giving or leaving assets to a favorite charity or to your community?

❑ What are your primary concerns and goals and why? What's really important to you?

FINANCIAL CONCERNS

❑ **Overall Planning**
   ❑ If you knew you only had six months to live, what changes would you make?

❑ **Wealth Creation**
   ❑ What is your overall investment strategy?
   ❑ How could you do a better job investing your personal, business, and retirement plan assets?
   ❑ Do you have the time, training, and temperament to manage your own investments?
   ❑ Is your life and disability insurance program adequate and cost effective?
   ❑ Are your investments and insurance coordinated with your overall goals?

❏ **Wealth Conservation**

    ❏ What changes should be made to your will or trust?

    ❏ What impact will estate taxes have on your family and business?

    ❏ What are the projected estate taxes? What could be done to reduce them?

    ❏ What would be the advantages of making gifts to your children?

    ❏ How would gifts to charity provide benefits to you and your family?

❏ **Business Continuation**

    ❏ What will happen to your business in the event of your death, disability, or retirement?

    ❏ How will you or your family ultimately get money out of the business?

- ❏ To what extent will your children be involved in the business? Who will run the business?
- ❏ Are your key managers adequately insured?
- ❏ If you sell the business, how should the sale be structured?

❏ **Executive Benefits**

- ☑ Are you providing yourself and your key managers with the most cost-effective fringe benefits?
- ☑ What are you doing to attract, retain, and reward key management?
- ❏ What impact would the loss of key management have on the business and on your plans?
- ❏ Do you have appropriate salary continuation plans and agreements?

FACTS AND FEELINGS

Tell me a little bit about yourself.

❑ How did you get started in this business?

❑ Why did you select this business?

❑ How much time do you spend working?

❑ How much vacation do you take? Who runs the business while you're gone?

❑ What makes your business unique?

❑ How is your business going now?

❑ Where do you see your business going over the next 5-10 years? Any problems?

❑ How do you hire and keep good people?

❏ What do you do in terms of any special rewards for your key people?

❏ What do you do to reward yourself?

❏ How much time do you spend with your family?

❏ What are your plans for your business when you retire or die?

❏ How will you get money out of your business for yourself or your family?

❏ Who will run the business?

❏ What are you doing for him or her that's special?

❏ What are you doing to discount the impact of estate taxes?

❑ How much time can you take off without it affecting your business?

❑ What are you doing about retirement?

❑ What are you doing for your community or for charity?

❑ How would you describe your investment results over the past five years? What would you have done differently?

❑ To what extent do you involve your attorney or accountant or any other advisor in your financial decisions?

GOALS

❑ **Considerations regarding retirement/financial independence:**

    ❑ At what age do you want to retire or be financially independent?

    ❑ How much income will you require (in today's dollars)?

    ❑ What inflation rate do you think is applicable?

    ❑ At retirement or termination of employment, what amount of money can you expect to receive from company retirement plan(s)? Other sources?

❑ **Considerations in the event of your death:**

    ❑ How much income do you want to provide your family?

    ❑ Will this include your spouse's earnings? How much?

- ❑ How much guaranteed income will your assets produce?
- ❑ After your children are grown, how much income do you want your spouse to have?
- ❑ Would you like your spouse to have the ability to pay off the mortgage?
- ❑ What other debts do you want paid off?
- ❑ How much money would you like to provide for your children's education?
- ❑ Do you feel your current life insurance program is adequate?
- ❑ How did you arrive at the amount of life insurance you have?

❏ **Considerations regarding estate planning:**
  ❏ What would be the amount of the estate taxes due at the death of you and your spouse?
  ❏ Do you want your family assets arranged to minimize estate taxes?
  ❏ Do you have a current will and/or trust arrangement?
  ❏ What was your purpose in creating the will or trust?
  ❏ Do you or your spouse anticipate an inheritance? How much?
  ❏ Have you made or considered making gifts to your children or charity?

❏ **Considerations regarding investing:**
  ❏ On a scale of 1-10 (1 being conservative and 10 speculative), how would you rank your past success as an investor?
  ❏ Do you have the time, desire and experience to select and manage your investments?
  ❏ Are there equities which are not available for investment purposes?
  ❏ What investments do you prefer (real estate, stocks, oil, etc.)?
  ❏ How much money do you have available to invest this year?
  ❏ How much money could you invest systematically monthly?

❏ **Other considerations or comments:**
  ❏ Are there any other goals or factors that you feel are important which would help us understand your priorities.

THE TOUGH QUESTIONS

❑ What are your feelings about life insurance?

❑ What is the purpose of your life insurance program?

❑ How do you feel about your children inheriting a large amount of money?

❑ If you were going to buy insurance in the future, why would you buy it?

❑ If insurance did not exist, what would you do?

❑ What do you think about term insurance?

❑ What do you think about buying term insurance and investing the difference?

❏ What do you think about cash value life insurance?

❏ What do you think about variable life insurance?

❏ What do you think about universal life?

❏ What do you like least about life insurance?

❏ When you bought insurance in the past, how did you determine the amount?

❏ How did you select the company and agent?

❏ Who was involved in the decision-making process?

❏ What is important to you?

❑ How do you want to be remembered by your children? Grandchildren? Employees?

❑ How much money do you feel you could save systematically on a monthly basis?

❑ If our analysis indicates that insurance is necessary to accomplish your goals, would there be any reason why you wouldn't go ahead with it?

❑ The question you really have to ask yourself is, "Do you care?"

❏ What are you doing to accumulate money on a systematic basis for your retirement?

❏ If insurance did not exist, what would you do to provide for your family in the event of your death?

❏ Do you have a cash cushion for your family and business to fall back on?

❏ Are you financially prepared to die or become disabled?

❏ Are you using pre-tax dollars to acquire your life insurance?

❏ If you were disabled, how long could your company afford to pay two people to do one person's work?

❏ Is your business paying for your life insurance?

❏ One day you are going to be unable to run your business. What happens then?

❏ One day you may not be here to take care of your family. What happens then?

❏ Would you like to guarantee your family's future or your business' future?

❏ Why don't I put together some options for you, so that you can take a look at them?

Personal Planning

- ❏ It's easy to say, "I love you." Life insurance means putting your money where your mouth is.

- ❏ Death is a ticking time bomb. You don't know when it is going to go off.

- ❏ Disability is a ticking time bomb.

- ❏ We don't have all the time in the world.

- ❏ Life insurance is a combination of caring, commitment and common sense.

- ❏ Income and net worth are no indication of financial expertise.

- ❏ The tough questions are the ones which you may not want to hear the answers to.

❏ If you were building a house, would you start with the roof or the chimney? Of course not. You would start with the foundation. It's the same thing with building a strong financial future for your family. You start with the foundation. Doesn't that make sense?

❏ A liability should not outlive the person who created it.

❏ You either have an estate tax problem, or an estate size problem.

❏ If your death will create an economic loss for your family, your business, your estate, your community, your church, your temple, your college, your school, or your favorite charity . . . then you probably need some life insurance.

❏ If you could only insure one . . . but not both . . . which would you insure, the golden eggs or the goose?

❏ If you had died last week, would your attorney or accountant take care of your family, or provide cash for your business, or pay the estate taxes?

❏ It's better to have insurance and not need it . . . than to need it and not have it.

❏ We all make mistakes. You can absorb little mistakes. Big mistakes can absorb you. A little mistake would be to buy life insurance and not need it. A big mistake would be to die without it. Wouldn't you agree?

❏ Do you know anyone who has too much cash?

❑ The best insurance is that which is in force when you die.

❑ It sounds to me as if you are running pretty hard. I hope you have a lot of life insurance.

❑ It's bad enough to die . . . don't do it for free.

❑ If the cost of getting an education is big, think of what the cost is for not getting one.

❑ It always feels good to do the right thing . . . just because it's the right thing to do. Wouldn't you agree?

❑ We help you design your future and your family's future today.

❏ With $200,000 worth of insurance, you must not plan on being dead very long.

❏ Life insurance works.

❏ There is no substitute for life insurance . . . not stocks, not bonds, not mutual funds, not real estate.

❏ There is no cost for having life insurance . . . only a cost for not having it.

❏ Someone always pays for life insurance whether or not it is bought. Either you pay for it or your family pays for it in terms of not having what you want them to have to remain in their world.

❑ Would you be interested in a plan where you get a million dollars at retirement or your family gets a million dollars if you don't make it to retirement?

❑ Some people know the price of everything and the value of nothing.

❑ The best time to buy life insurance is today. You would have been better off buying it yesterday, but that is no longer an option.

❑ There is absolutely no advantage to waiting to buy life insurance. Your health may change. You may die. The cost increases, the benefits decrease. Right now you hold all the cards.

❑ Plan for tomorrow, then focus on today.

❏ Is the uninsured life worth living?

❏ Do you have a lease on life?

❏ No one has a lease on life. If you don't die before age 65 . . . you will die after age 65.

❏ I don't know. What do you think?

❏ Why is it that the obvious is never obvious?

❏ Life insurance is just plain common sense . . . but common sense is uncommon.

❏ It always makes sense to have a cash cushion, because you don't want your money to run out before you do. You don't want to outlive your money.

❏ You don't buy life insurance because you're going to die. You buy it because you want your family to continue to live in the world that you've created together.

❏ Are you planning on taking your standard of living with you?

❏ It's tough enough living within your income. How will your family live without your income? How would you live without your income?

❏ Insurance poor? You don't become poor by buying life insurance. Your family could become poor if you don't.

❏ When was the last time you had a call from your attorney or your accountant with a good idea?

❏ Regardless of when you die . . . there's always a need for cash.

❏ Job A pays $100,000 per year. It pays nothing if you are disabled. Job B pays $98,000 per year. It pays $60,000 per year if you are disabled. Which job would you prefer?

❏ If the worst investment you ever made resulted in your getting back four times your original investment or your family getting ten times your original investment in the event of your death, wouldn't you feel pretty good about that?

❏ Why do successful people buy more life insurance? They have more to lose, and they recognize their value and responsibility to others.

❏ The cost of permanent cash value life insurance is not the premium. It is part of the interest you might have earned if you had systematically invested the money elsewhere. If you keep the policy until you die, there is no cost for having it. There would be a huge cost for not having it.

❏ Money will not offset the emotional loss, but it will help reduce the economic loss. A great economic loss can make the emotional loss even greater.

❏ The only real security is that which you provide for yourself.

❏ Should you buy insurance? Will there be an economic loss to someone or something when you die?

❏ How do you mean that?

❏ Could you elaborate on that?

❏ Why do you say that?

❏ Why?

❏ Circumstances change. It never hurts to get a second opinion. No one has covered all the bases. No one has a corner on good ideas.

❏ Have you ever made a bad investment? Tell me about it.

❏ With life insurance, if you make a mistake and don't have enough, it's your family who pays the price.

❏ There are basically two types of people . . . those who care and those who don't. Which are you?

- ❏ It's the right thing to do . . . and you can afford it.

- ❏ Insurance is like a parachute. You have to have it before you need it.

- ❏ Investing $10,000 per year, how long would it take you to accumulate $1,000,000?

- ❏ There are some things you just have to have regardless of the rate of return because they are necessary. Life insurance and medical insurance and disability insurance are among those things. Wouldn't you agree?

- ❏ Life insurance is just putting money away for a rainy day, which is just good old-fashioned common sense. Wouldn't you agree?

❏ Money is worth no more than what it costs to borrow. Key people make it worth 15% or 20%.

❏ How much of what you own isn't yours?

❏ If it makes sense to insure against an *improbable* loss such as your car, home or jewelry . . . wouldn't it make sense to insure against an *inevitable* loss?

❏ When you die, would your family be better off with $1,000,000 of the most costly insurance or $100,000 of the least costly insurance?

❏ Don't trust your family's financial future to luck.

❏ How long can you afford to be dead? How long can you afford to be disabled?

❏ If you live, it's a savings plan. When you die, it's insurance . . . a tax-free cash cushion for your family to fall back on.

❏ Isn't there someone or a favorite charity that you would like to leave some money to? Life insurance will enable you to leverage your legacy.

❏ It takes more than money to buy life insurance. It takes good health and character.

❏ Life insurance is really lifestyle insurance. It enables your family to remain in the world you have created together.

❏ Most people want security and peace of mind. That's what insurance provides.

- No one ever dies at the right time. They always have unfinished dreams. Life insurance will help keep your dreams alive.

- Perhaps you can say you don't need life insurance, but can you really say for certain that your family won't need it?

- Plan and live each day as if it were your last. One day it will be.

- There are only two ways to convert your dreams to reality: one is to live and the other is to insure.

- It's not how much you earn, it's how much you keep that counts.

- Why don't you sleep on it? If you wake up, give me a call.

Estate Planning

❏ Estate taxes are a ticking time bomb.

❏ Would you rather have your estate go to your children or to 250,000,000 strangers?

❏ Do you think that the IRS will put up a building with your name on it?

❏ Do you think that your children's paying estate taxes will build character?

❏ Would you rather have $5,000,000 go to the IRS estate tax collector or $1,000,000 go to the insurance company?

❏ Wouldn't you rather use my money than your money to pay what has to be paid to the IRS tax collector (or to the bank)?

❏ If you can't pay 1% a year during your lifetime, how will your children pay 100% plus when you are gone?

❏ If you can't pay the interest only, how will your children pay both principal and interest?

❏ If you'll pay the interest, we'll provide the principal.

❏ It's not how much you leave . . . but how much is left that counts.

❏ Why not let the event that creates the problem also create the solution?

❏ Why not use 1% of your estate growth to protect the other 99% of your estate? For example, if your estate grows at 10% a year and your estate is worth $10,000,000, why not use $100,000 of that growth to purchase $5,000,000 of insurance to pay the estate tax? Why not let 1% of your estate protect the other 99%?

❏ If you'll give me 1% of your estate each year, I will pay your estate tax. Wouldn't it make sense to let 1% of your estate protect the other 99%?

❏ Give me $1. I will put $5 in a special account for your children. If you keep the $1, only 50¢ will get to your children. My way they get $5. Your way they get 50¢. Which plan do you prefer?

❏ How do you create a small fortune? Subject a large fortune to estate taxes.

❑ When it comes to wills and estate plans, most people either don't have one or it's out of date.

❑ There's never too much money . . . only too little character.

❑ Attorneys distribute dollars. We create the dollars to be distributed.

❑ Regarding Section 6166, how would you like to be in partnership with the IRS?

❑ Section 6166 does not provide the cash to pay the tax. What it does is to provide for the installment payment of the tax. This means paying principal plus interest. Why not pay interest only . . . rather than principal plus interest?

❏ Which assets have you earmarked to pay estate taxes?

❏ As a business person, if you knew that you faced an inevitable loss which you could discount by 80% or more, wouldn't it make sense to explore that option?

❏ May I show you how much of what you own you really don't own? (Show Estate Tax Chart.)

❏ The tax law will continue to change. What doesn't change is the need for cash to pay the estate tax.

❏ Would you like to reduce the cost of paying estate taxes by 80% or more?

❏ Your estate is the tangible representation of your lifetime. Why spend a lifetime building it if overnight you are going to let the IRS take it apart? If it makes sense to build it, wouldn't it make sense to keep it?

❏ Given a choice among your children, charity, or the IRS estate tax collector, where would you want your estate to go, in order of priority?

❏ If you purchase the insurance and they do away with the estate tax, which is unlikely, that just means your children, grandchildren, and favorite charity will get more money. Everyone wins. How does that sound?

❏ In any event, there will still be substantial income taxes to be paid on the money in qualified and non-qualified retirement plans, IRA's, and variable or fixed annuities.

Business Planning

❏ If you were to die tonight, what would happen to your business? Who would run it? What income would your family receive? Would your banker be your primary beneficiary?

❏ Are you insuring your PC's for more than your VP's?

❏ If a person is key to his business, isn't he key to his family?

❏ How would you feel about being in business with your partner's wife . . . or rather his widow? And her children? And her attorney? And her new husband? And his children? And his attorney?

❏ If your banker said it would cost 11% rather than 10% to borrow $1,000,000, would you still borrow the money? Of course you would. The extra 1% would ensure your company's ability to repay the loan in the event you're not there to do it.

❏ Why not let 1% of the value of your business protect the other 99%?

❏ Why not let 1% of your sales protect the other 99%?

❏ The best fringe benefit you can provide your employees is a continuing job when you die.

❏ Do you want your business to die when you do?

❏ What are you doing to reward and retain your key employees?

❏ Would you like to be able to reward Tom, without also having to reward Dick and Harry?

❏ Would you be interested in a plan which would provide you with $1,000,000 at your retirement, or $1,000,000 for your family if you die prior to retirement . . . all at no cost to your company?

❏ If someone offered you $1,000,000, would you be interested?

❏ There are certain things your business can do for you more effectively than you can do them.

❑ Do you ever take any vacation? For how long? Do you call your office? How often? Who runs your business while you're gone? How long could you be gone and not call without it affecting your business? What if you went on vacation and never returned?

❑ What would happen to your business if you were to die tonight?

❑ 20% return? Are you getting 20% on your cash reserves? Do you have an unused line of credit?

Term Insurance

❏ Term is an option on tomorrow.

❏ Buying term and investing the difference is like running a marathon. In a marathon, you can be ahead for 26 miles, and if you fall behind in the last few hundred yards, you still lose. It's the same thing with buying term and investing the difference. You can be ahead by buying term and investing the difference for 10 or 15 years, but when you fall behind, you still lose, regardless of how long you were ahead.

❏ Term insurance represents an increasing liability. Permanent insurance represents an increasing asset. Which would you rather have?

❏ Death is a permanent problem. Term insurance is a temporary solution. Less than 20% of people die before age 65.

❏ The longer you live, the more apt you are to drop term insurance. It will have been money down the drain for nothing.

❏ The only way to win with term insurance is to get lucky and die soon. Most people wouldn't consider that lucky.

❏ There is only one problem with term insurance. It doesn't work . . . unless you get lucky.

❏ With term insurance, the only way you can win is to lose. You have to die soon. Otherwise the premium is like a stairway to nowhere. It goes up and up and up until it gets to the point where you can't hang on and you can't let go.

❏ It does not matter how little you pay for something if it doesn't work.

- ❏ What is the rate of return on your car? Why not buy a VW and invest the difference?

- ❏ Why not buy less expensive clothes and invest the difference?

- ❏ Why not buy less expensive furniture and invest the difference?

- ❏ Why not dine out less frequently and invest the difference? .

- ❏ With term insurance, most people end up having paid a lot for nothing. Ultimately, you stop paying because the premium just keeps going up. The only way you can win with term is to die.

- ❏ Wouldn't you rather save or invest money than spend it?

Objections and
Responses

- ❏ I'M NOT INTERESTED.

- ❏ Why?

- ❏ Why is that?

- ❏ Why do you say that?

- ❏ What do you mean?

- ❏ What is it that you're not interested in?

- ❏ I really did not expect you to be interested until I have shown you some ideas which might make sense to you.

- ❏ I can understand your feeling that way. Many of my clients initially felt exactly the same way, but they found that I could make and save them a lot of money.

❏ I DON'T WANT TO SPEND THAT MUCH MONEY ON LIFE INSURANCE.

❏ You're not spending money. You're saving it. You're just moving money from your right pocket to your left pocket. From one bank to another type of bank.

❏ Let's put the premium and the problem in perspective. The premium is peanuts compared to the problem. It's only 1% of the problem. If you can't afford the premium, how will your family or business be able to afford the problem?

❏ How much do you feel you can afford to save or invest?

❏ I WANT TO BUY TERM IN-
SURANCE AND INVEST THE
DIFFERENCE.

❏ Great. Why don't we get started with
the term insurance for now so that
you will have the insurance locked in,
and we can discuss converting to
permanent insurance later? Doesn't
that make sense?

❏ I can understand your feeling that way
because many of my clients felt exactly
the same way. However, when they
took a closer look at the numbers, they
decided term did not really measure up.
Let's take a look at the numbers.

❏ GOD WILL TAKE CARE OF MY
FAMILY.

❏ That's why I'm here.

❑ I'M NOT WORRIED ABOUT DYING.

❑ No one has a lease on life. If you don't die before age 65 . . . you will die after age 65.

❑ MY WIFE CAN SELL THE HOME AND SHE AND THE KIDS CAN MOVE INTO A SMALLER ONE.

❑ If your wife had died, would you sell your home and move into a smaller one? Of course not. Then why should she have to?

❑ I WANT TO LOOK AT SOME OTHER NUMBERS FROM SOME OTHER COMPANIES.

❑ I've taken the liberty of getting some other quotes for you. Would you like to take a look at them? The reasons I'm recommending ABC Life are:

- ❏ History of low cost over the long haul
- ❏ Financial integrity
- ❏ Financial strength
- ❏ Strong backup if something happens to me

❏ I'VE ALWAYS DONE ALL MY BUSINESS WITH XYZ LIFE.

❏ Wouldn't it make sense to diversify? If you had a million dollars to invest, would you put it all in IBM stock? Of course not. Wouldn't it make sense to diversify your insurance portfolio also?

❑ I JUST DON'T CARE WHAT HAPPENS WHEN I'M GONE. THAT'S THEIR PROBLEM.

❑ Good-bye. (A caring, responsible person would not think that, let alone say it.)

❑ Are you saying that because I am a life insurance agent, and you're afraid I might sell you some life insurance, or do you really mean it?

❑ You don't mean that. (This is for someone who is willing to get into a discussion of one's responsibilities to others.)

❑ I HAVE TOO MUCH INSURANCE
NOW.

❑ Let's review your goals for your family
and your business.

❑ I'M NOT GOING TO BUY ANY
MORE LIFE INSURANCE.

❑ Why do you say that?

❑ I can't create a need for life insurance.
You either need it based on your goals
for your family and your business, or
you don't. Why don't we briefly
review your situation?

❑ I won't recommend it unless you need
it based on your goals. Isn't that fair?

❏ TIMING IS BAD. BUSINESS IS
 DOWN. I WANT TO WAIT.

❏ Why don't we go ahead now with the
 term insurance, which costs peanuts.
 Let's get the insurance locked in so that
 you hold all the cards. If you wait, your
 health might change or you might die.
 In any event, waiting means your age
 will increase, which means the cost
 increases and the benefits decrease.

❏ THIS IS TOO COMPLEX.

❏ Where am I not making myself clear?

❏ Let's review the major points and how
 this plan accomplishes your goals.

❑ YOUR PRICE IS TOO HIGH.

❑ Price is what you pay going in. Cost is what you pay over the long haul.

❑ Over the long haul, we have always been one of the most competitive companies in the industry.

❑ You don't want the low-cost bidder when it comes to parachutes, life preservers, and life insurance.

❑ Do you want the lowest price or the best value? Value encompasses a lot of things: ideas, solutions, benefits, price and cost, quality, integrity, service, and communication. Are those things important to you?

- ❏ YOUR COMPETITION HAS A BETTER PRODUCT.

- ❏ In what way?

- ❏ Let's compare them side by side. Let's look at history.

- ❏ WE'RE EXPECTING TOUGH TIMES. I WANT TO WAIT.

- ❏ Insurance is just what you need to get through tough times.

- ❏ Are you concerned about cash flow? Why don't we get started with the term insurance?

- ❏ I'M INSURANCE POOR.

- ❏ What do you mean?

❏ I'M SORRY, BUT I'M NOT GOING TO DO BUSINESS WITH YOU.

❏ Why is that? Where did I go wrong? Is there anything that I can do to get things back on track?

❏ Circumstances change. Would you have any objection to my keeping in touch from time to time?

❏ I WANT TO DISCUSS THIS WITH MY WIFE (ATTORNEY, ACCOUNT-ANT, ETC.).

❏ Isn't this really your decision to make?

❏ What is it that you want to discuss with her?

❏ If it were up to you, what action would you take?

❏ What are you going to do if she says no?

❏ Why don't we set a time for the three of us to get together? She will undoubtedly have some questions which you and I have not discussed.

❏ Why would you ask your attorney or your accountant if you love your family or if you want your lifetime liquidated?

❏ Will your attorney or your accountant provide cash for your family or business?

❏ I WANT TO THINK IT OVER.

❏ Why?

❏ What is it that you want to think over?
    ❏ Is it doing business with ABC Life?
    ❏ Is it me? Are you comfortable doing business with me?
    ❏ Is it the amount of insurance?
    ❏ Is it the type of insurance? Whether it's term or permanent?
    ❏ Is it the premium?

❏ I can understand your wanting to think it over. Why don't you think it over while I step outside for a few minutes (or take a walk around the block). While I'm gone, why don't you write down any questions or concerns that you may have so that we can discuss them when I return.

❏ While you're thinking it over, why not let us think it over? It will take about two months to see if you can qualify. From the time I deliver the policy to you . . . you have another ten days to think it over and still get your money back. You have nothing to lose by going ahead now.

❏ While you're thinking it over . . . why don't we get started on finding out if you can qualify. Right now you really have nothing to think over.

❏ There is no risk on your part by going ahead. You will have plenty of time to think it over. In fact, from the time I deliver the policy to you, you will then have 10 days in which to think it over and still get all your money back. That's fair, isn't it?

Closing the Sale

❑ Which plan do you prefer?

❑ Put me on your payroll for $10 per hour ($20,000 per year, based on 40 hours per week, 50 weeks per year, or 2,000 hours). When you walk out, I'll walk in with $1,000,000 at the time when it's needed most. Ten years downstream, if you want to call the deal off, I will give you all your money back plus interest. Put me on your payroll. Wouldn't that make sense?

❑ Why don't I have the doctor's office give you a call in order to set up a medical exam . . . which, of course, will be at our expense . . . so that we can get started on the paperwork to see if you qualify? All I need is your okay on a few pieces of paper.

❏ Wouldn't we all look stupid if something happens to you or your health
changes while this is in underwriting?
Let's put the insurance in effect. All I
need is a check.

❏ All I need is your okay on a few pieces
of paper . . . and a check.

❏ All I need is a check.

❏ While I'm filling out these forms . . .
why don't you make a check payable to
ABC Life in the amount of $4,000.

❏ What do you think?

❏ What do you like most about this plan?

❏ Put me on your payroll.

❏ Why do I need a check? Because it's customary. It shifts the risk from you, your family, and your business . . . to the insurance company.

❏ The premium is not the problem. The premium is the solution to the problem.

❏ Compared to the problem . . . the premium is always peanuts.

❏ You must have a good reason for saying that. Do you mind if I ask you what it is?

❏ Which check would you rather sign? $5,000,000 to the IRS or $100,000 for ten years to the insurance company?

❑ If you owned a printing press capable of printing legal, spendable U.S. dollars at the rate of $200,000 per year, would you insure the printing press? Of course you would. For how much?

❑ If you wait for all the lights to turn green, you'll never get started.

❑ If there is a need for life insurance to accomplish your goals, is there any reason why we can't do business together?

❑ You need two things . . . the plan and the money. The plan without the money won't work. The money without a plan might work. Let's get the money first . . . and then work out the details.

❑ You're not spending money. You're saving it. You're just transferring capital from one bank to another type of bank. This special bank will give you higher interest over the long haul, and it's tax deferred. This special bank's plan is self-completing in the event of death or disability. If you asked your regular banker for the same deal, he would laugh. He can't do it.

❑ How much does it cost to move money from your left pocket to your right pocket? How much does it cost to move money from one bank to another bank?

❑ We're just repositioning your assets to give you more leverage.

❑ Regarding competition . . . you don't want the low cost bid on parachutes, life preservers, or life insurance.

❑ You agreed that you needed life insurance when you thought you were in perfect health. Doesn't it make even more sense when you've found out that you're not in perfect health?

❑ If the insurance company thought you were going to die soon, they wouldn't issue a policy. What they're saying is that statistically, they think you might die at 70 rather than 75.

❑ What do you mean you're not going to buy anything?

❏ Let's look at the bottom line. Let's pretend that you are now age 65 and you are looking back at your options at age 35. Which plan would you wish you had chosen? Plan A, you'll have paid $110,000 for nothing. Plan B, you will have invested an additional $40,000 and you'll have $1,000,000 of ongoing insurance or $377,000 in cash. Which plan do you prefer?

❏ If you can't afford to be without the premium, how can your family or business afford to be without the benefits?

❏ Regarding your life insurance program, if you make a mistake, it's your family who pays the price.

❏ Do you always buy the cheapest things? Of course not. Why would you want to do that with your life insurance?

❏ Isn't your family's financial security worth $_____ per month?

❏ It doesn't matter how little it costs if it does not do the job.

❏ All I need is a check. Would you prefer to do this on an annual or monthly basis?

❏ Do you want me to be direct . . . or diplomatic?

❏ Do you want me to tell you what you want to hear or should I tell you what you need to hear?

❏ If you are wrong . . . what happens then? Your family will pay a big price. The premium is peanuts.

❏

+	−
• $1,000,000 for your retirement • $1,000,000 for your family • Cash reserve • Self-completing if you're disabled	• Premium = Peanuts • $10 per hour

Miscellaneous

REASONS PEOPLE DON'T BUY

The reasons people don't buy basically boil down to the following:

- ❏ No Money
- ❏ No Caring
- ❏ No Understanding
- ❏ No Need
- ❏ No Trust
- ❏ No Hurry

❏ **No Money.** By doing a proper fact and feeling-finding interview, you will learn the prospect's assets, liabilities, and cash flow, so that you are not recommending something the individual cannot afford. How can you really recommend the right amount of insurance if you don't know these things anyhow? The prospect will normally think the premium is coming out of his personal cash flow and will diminish his current standard of living. In reality, the premium is almost always a capital transfer, and it often involves the repositioning of corporate capital.

❏ **No Caring.** Would you rather find out after five minutes or five hours whether someone cares? People who don't care, don't buy life insurance. If there is a need for life insurance in order to accomplish your goals, is there any reason why you would not be willing to do business with me?

❏ **No Understanding.** Most people don't buy what they don't understand. The responsibility for communicating lies with you as the salesperson. Don't try to impress people with complex concepts and jargon. It is easy to make something complex. The beauty lies in reducing a complex concept to simplicity. If they don't buy the concept, the details are irrelevant.

❏ **No Need.** When someone dies, their death will almost invariably create an economic loss. There will be a need for cash in one or more of these areas:

Personal Planning
    ❏ Income Continuation
    ❏ Estate Tax Funding
    ❏ Special Bequests

Business Planning
    ❏ Buy & Sell Funding
    ❏ Key Management Loss
    ❏ Selective Benefits

Other parts of this book will help you pinpoint the problems.

❏ **No Trust.** First, you have to be trust-worthy. You have to trust yourself. You have to place your client's interest before your own. You have to believe that what you are recommending is the right thing for your client to do. It is what you would do if you were in his shoes.

❏ **No Hurry.** Waiting accomplishes nothing. The best time to buy is now. If you wait, your health might change or you might die. In any event, your age will increase, which means the cost increases and the benefits decrease. Let's get started with the paperwork. Let's find out if you can qualify while you still hold all the cards.

PRE-APPROACH LETTER

(Staple a crisp, new $1 bill to this letter.)

Robert Sample
Apex Corporation
123 Main Street
Anywhere, CA 94104

Dear Mr. Sample:

Attached to this letter is a tax-free dollar. Within the next ten days, I will call you to arrange an appointment to show you how other successful individuals are using tax-free and tax-deferred dollars to:

- ❏ Enhance their own retirement income
- ❏ Maximize their pension benefits
- ❏ Protect their families
- ❏ Discount the impact of estate taxes
- ❏ Leverage their gifts to charity
- ❏ Facilitate the continuation of their businesses
- ❏ Reward their key employees

I genuinely look forward to meeting you.

Sincerely yours,

W. Howard Wight, Jr.
Chartered Financial Consultant

P.S. Tom Jones, for whom I recently did some planning, suggested that I contact you.

ASKING FOR REFERRALS

Mr. Client, I need your help. As you recall, Jack Jones referred me to you. Would you be willing to help me meet other successful, responsible people like yourself? Don't try to guess whether they need life insurance. Your referring me will enable me to meet them on a favorable basis.

Who do you know? Why don't we go through your personal phone directory as a starting point? Your referring me to other people enables me to provide you with better service because I have to spend less time prospecting.

WHO:
- ❏ Owns a Business
- ❏ Is a Partner in a Business
- ❏ May be Starting a Business
- ❏ Owns a Lot of Real Estate

- ❏ Has a Lot of Investments
- ❏ May Inherit Sizeable Funds
- ❏ Is a Top Salesperson
- ❏ Is a Top Executive with a Successful Company
- ❏ Is Successful and Responsible and Growing

SOURCES OF NAMES:
- ❏ Family, Friends, Neighbors
- ❏ Business Associates
- ❏ Suppliers, Customers, Competitors
- ❏ Attorneys and Accountants
- ❏ Physicians and Dentists
- ❏ Association and Club Directories
- ❏ Business Card File
- ❏ Rolodex
- ❏ Personal Phone Directory

SOURCES OF PREMIUM AND INVESTMENT DOLLARS

- ❏ Sell Poorly Performing Investments
- ❏ Margin Securities
- ❏ Split Dollar
- ❏ Late-Start Split Dollar
- ❏ Executive Bonus Plan
- ❏ Exchange Policy (Section 1035)
- ❏ Home Equity Loan
- ❏ Loan from Qualified Plans, Other Investments, Relatives
- ❏ Sell Assets
- ❏ Tax Savings
- ❏ Surrender Old Policies (be aware of tax consequences)
- ❏ Change Dividend Option on Insurance Policies
- ❏ Surrender Paid-Up Additions of Old Policies
- ❏ Borrow from Old Policies
- ❏ Put Old Policies on Paid-Up Basis
- ❏ Corporation as Source
- ❏ 401(k)
- ❏ Profit Sharing
- ❏ Pension
- ❏ _____
- ❏ _____
- ❏ _____

114

VALUE CONSISTS OF:

- ❏ IDEAS
- ❏ SOLUTIONS
- ❏ BENEFITS
- ❏ PRICE
- ❏ COST
- ❏ QUALITY
- ❏ INTEGRITY
- ❏ SERVICE
- ❏ COMMUNICATION

Which of these are important to you?

"It's unwise to pay too much, but it's worse to pay too little. When you pay too much, you lose a little money . . . that is all. When you pay too little, you sometimes lose everything, because the thing you bought was incapable of doing the thing it was bought to do. The common law of business balance prohibits paying a little and getting a lot. It can't be done. If you deal with the lowest bidder, it is well to add something for the risk you run, and if you do that . . . you will have enough to pay for something better."

JOHN RUSKIN

ABOUT THE AUTHOR

Born in Baltimore, Maryland, Howard Wight graduated from the U.S. Naval Academy in 1961 and served with the Navy Seabees in Vietnam. He joined Connecticut General in 1969 in San Francisco.

Howard was an agent with Northwestern Mutual from 1973-1990. In 1983, he started publishing the Wight Financial Concepts Newsletter, to which many of the top insurance and financial advisors in the country subscribe.

Howard Wight conducts about 50 seminars annually on selling, motivation, success, and time management. He has been a featured speaker at the Million Dollar Round Table annual meeting five times and at the International Forum twice.

He is the author of seven books including *Success and Time Management* and *Life Insurance in a Nutshell*.

Howard Wight
Wight Financial Concepts Corporation
1330 Jones Street, Suite 404
San Francisco, CA 94109
800-486-SELL
www.HowardWight.com